LIVIN' DE LIFE

A Play for Young People

by

Ed Graczyk

Suggested by the tales and characters recorded in
Joel Chandler Harris'
"The Uncle Remus Tales"

ROYALTY NOTE

The possession of this book, without a written authorization first having been obtained from the publisher, confers no right or license, to professionals or amateurs, to produce the play, publicly or in private, for gain or charity.

In its present form, this play is dedicated to the reading public only, and not to producers. However, productions of this play are encouraged, and those who wish to present it may secure the necessary permission by writing to The Anchorage Press, Cloverlot, Anchorage, Kentucky 40223.

Professional producers are requested to apply to The Anchorage Press for royalty quotation.

This play may be presented by amateurs, upon payment to The Anchorage Press, of a royalty of $25.00 for each performance, one week before the date the play is to be given. The play is fully protected by copyright, and anyone presenting the play without the consent of The Anchorage Press, will be liable to the penalties provided by the copyright law.

Whenever the play is produced, the name of the author must be carried in all publicity, advertising, fliers, and programmes. Also the following notice must appear on all printed programmes: "Produced by special arrangement with The Anchorage Press, of Anchorage, Kentucky."

THE CHARACTERS
(in order of appearance)

BRER TARRYPIN

BRER COON

BRER RABBIT

BRER FOX

BRER BEAR

MISS MEADOWS

AUNT MAMMY-BAMMY

SIS BUZZARD

MISS GOOSE

THE PLACE
The Briar Patch

The premiere performance of *Livin' de Life* was given 6 August, 1970, by the Pickwick Players of the Midland Community Theatre in Midland, Texas. Following is a copy of the programme:

The Pickwick Players

of Midland Community Theatre

Present

The World Premiere Production of

LIVIN' DE LIFE

by ED GRACZYK

Designed and Directed by

ED GRACZYK

The Cast:

BRER TARRYPIN	Bill Thomas
BRER COON	Ken Kubic
BRER RABBIT	Jimmy Heck
BRER FOX	Ted Caryl
BRER BEAR	Conrad Coffield
MISS MEAODWS	Ann Thomas
AUNT MAMMY-BAMMY	Lucinda Huffman
SIS BUZZARD	Diana McCants
MISS GOOSE	Bonnie Cooper
DOC CROW	Jim Hankinson

Production Staff:

Publicity	MARION MCINTYRE
Stage Manager	NANCY MATHYS
Assistant Stage Manager	JIM HANKINSON
Lights	GERRY PYLE
Sound	MIKE COFFIELD
Masks executed by	JIM WALTERS
Box Office	ANN THOMAS
Costumes	JIM WALTERS
	NANCY MATHYS
	BONNIE COOPER
	FRANCIS PEACOCK
	MARION PEACOCK
Props	NATALIE HARMON
	MARY MACINA
	JULIE BROWN
Construction	MARK SKRABACZ and
	PICKWICK BOYS

4

"LIVIN' DE LIFE"

FOREWORD

The stories dramatized in this play are very old. Joel Chandler Harris, author of "Animal Stories", published in 1880, served merely as collector and recorder of a delightful group of folk tales which were at that time, according to Harris in the introduction of his book, already "a part of the domestic history of every Southern family". His stated purpose was that of literary historian, ". . . to preserve the legends themselves in their original simplicity".

Like Harris, I also believe in the value of preserving these charming folk tales which are such an important and enchanting part of our nation's heritage. "LIVIN' DE LIFE!" presents the Br'er Rabbit stories in an exciting, contemporary form to still another generation of American young people.

A modified version of the dialect recorded by Harris has been retained in "LIVIN' DE LIFE!" in order to capture the unique flavor of the original tales. It is not intended to represent a Negro dialect and should not be interpreted as such by the actors; rather, it is a more universal type of speech as might have been spoken by many back-woods or country folk. The dialect, combined with the animal costumes and rural setting, sets the animals apart from the ordniary and every-day and makes them special. Br'er Rabbit, Br'er Fox, Br'er Bear and the rest of the critters could not speak in any other way and remain true to the mood and feeling of the original folk tales.

The philosophies handed down by word of mouth and recorded by Joel Chandler Harris are as valid today as they were in 1880 and before. "LIVIN' DE LIFE!" preserves and presents these philosophies for today's youth in still another form, a play for young people anywhere.

So quit worryin' about de worries an' start "LIVIN' DE LIFE!"

Ed Graczyk

Livin' de Life, as produced by Pickwick Players, of Midland, Texas

LIVIN' DE LIFE

The sounds of night combined with a peaceful melody played on a harmonica. The curtain rises slowly to reveal the set. It is early morning on a summer day. The set is simple in structure but complex in richness of mood. Mood is very important to the play. As the play moves through the countryside, this simple structure with a minimum of changes will suggest the locale.

Center stage elevated about four feet is a footbridge with crudely constructed side rails. Leading to the stage floor on both sides of the bridge are two sections of ramps. The upstage sections lead directly to the wings; the downstage ramps sweep in a curve toward center stage. One may reach the bridge from upstage or downstage. These ramps should be elevated on stilts and not faced solidly, so the actors may hide beneath them and also to give the set an open, airy quality. Tall grass, reeds and cattails grow up from the base of the ramps. Along the upstage side of the ramps are groups of tall poles at various heights. Several of these are trees; one stage right has a beehive hanging from it, to be used later in the play. The remaining poles have lighting instruments attached to them; these instruments will supply all of our mood lighting. They should be exposed at all times, and not hidden by trees.

Along the base of the poles are several bushes used for hiding. This combination of pieces should have the appearance of a single unit . . . airy, solid, non-realistic and beautiful in detail.

At the beginning, shafts of blue and green light flood the stage from the light poles, while the stage is bathed lightly in golden yellow from the area lights.

As the curtain rises, we see Brer Tarrypin sitting at the base of one of the stage right trees, playing a harmonica. Brer Coon sits on the bridge, his legs dangling over the edge, whittling. The mood is quiet, peaceful and serene as the pole lights slowly cross fade to the yellow and orange of daytime. The sun, a large round cardboard cut-out, is slowly raised. Birds begin to sing and suddenly, from off-left, the mood is broken by the screams and wails of Brer Fox and Brer Bear. The music builds in tempo, as onstage runs Brer Rabbit, with Brer Fox and Brer Bear in hot pursuit. Brer Bear carries a huge club.

BRER COON (*To Brer Rabbit as he runs by*). De prankin' an' de caperin' has started mighty early today . . . hasn't dey, Brer Rabbit?

(The entire chase is almost mechanical; its the same thing every day. Brer Rabbit runs up the ramp, across the bridge and down left. He stops, breathes heavily, and waits for Brer Fox and Brer Bear to catch up. They stop on the bridge, fan themselves with

their hats, and proceed. Brer Rabbit runs under the bridge and up the up right ramp to the bridge. Brer Coon hands him a handkerchief; he wipes his brow, runs down the down left ramp and hides under the bridge. At the bridge, Brer Coon mechanically points off left. They run off left. When they are gone, Brer Rabbit comes out of hiding).

BRER RABBIT. Thanks again, Brer Coon.

BRER COON. Did it last time . . . do de same next time, Brer Rabbit.

BRER RABBIT. Well, dere ain't gonna be a next time no more.

BRER TERRYPIN. What you sayin', Brer Rabbit? You ain't gonna give in to dose two varmints, are ya?

BRER RABBIT. I have had it! I'm plum tuckered out from caperin' with dose two. I set myself down with myself and together we had a good long talk 'bout it . . . an' we've decided!

BRER COON. What did you'se decide, brer Rabbit?

BRER RABBIT. We decided to leave de Briar Patch for good an' for always!

BRER TARRYPIN AND BRER COON. Leave de Briar Patch!

BRER RABBIT. Dat's right!

BRER TARRYPIN. Why, you been cuttin' capers with dose two ever since I can remember. Dey keeps tryin' to ketch you and you keeps escapin' and pullin' new capers.

BRER COON *(Chuckles).* Yes, sir . . . you sure has a knack of stirrin' up de mischief . . . I think you just run outa new capers, dat's what I think.

(He chuckles again).

BRER RABBIT. No, sir, I mean it! I'm gonna leave de troubles an' de problems behind! An' together, me an' myself, we're headin' for a new place!

BRER COON. It'll be kinda dull an' quiet without ya, Brer Rabbit.

BRER RABBIT. Well, I've decided, and dat's what I'm gonna do . . . unless, you two can come up with another solution to de problem.

BRER TARRYPIN *(Chuckles).* Yes, sir . . . you *got* it, all right!

BRER RABBIT. What I got, Brer Tarrypin?

BRER TARRYPIN. You've gone an' conjured up yourself a bad case of de Mopes.

BRER RABBIT. What's de Mopes? Is it serious? . . . come to think of it, I have been scratchin' a lot lately . . .

(He scratches. Brer Tarrypin laughs).

What you laughin' at Brer Tarrypin? . . . am I turnin' colors?
. . . what color is de Mopes?

BRER TARRYPIN. De Mopes don't have no color, Brer Rabbit.

BRER RABBIT. Oh, a no-color disease . . . dose is de worst kind!

(He groans and aches all over).

I think it's gettin' de best of me now . . .

(Groans).

Dere it is, sneakin' in de back way to get me for good!

(Brer Tarrypin and Brer Coon are doubled over with laughter).

. . . What are you two laughin' at? . . . I am ailin'!

BRER TARRYPIN. I think for once somethin's got the best of you, Brer
Rabbit. De Mopes ain't no disease.

BRER RABBIT *(His old self again)*. Dey ain't? Den what is dey?

BRER TARRYPIN. De Mopes is a feelin' . . . it's kinda hard to describe
. . . but I got a notion dat once you get over de Mopes, you'll be
just fine.

BRER RABBIT. Is dere a cure for de Mopes? How long's it take?

BRER TARRYPIN. Kinda hard to say . . . may take a day . . . maybe a
week . . . maybe two.

BRER RABBIT. Well, if anyone can cure de Mopes, I think I know
who can . . .

(He starts to dash off).

See ya later!

BRER COON. Where ya rushin' off to, Brer Rabbit?

BRER RABBIT. I'm headed for de Creepy Crawly Forest an' pay me
a visit on old Aunt Mammy-Bammy. She'll find me a cure for
de Mopes, sure enough!

BRER TARRYPIN. Good idea, Brer Rabbit . . . an' be sure an' give old
Aunt Mammy a howdy for me.

BRER RABBIT. Sure will, Brer Tarrypin.

(Miss Meadows enters).

Mornin', Miss Meadows.

MISS MEADOWS. Mornin', Brer Rabbit . . . where you off to in such
a hurry?

BRER RABBIT. Don't get too close or ya might ketch it!

MISS MEADOWS. Ketch what?

Brer Tarrypin. Brer Rabbit has gone an' caught himself a bad case of de Mopes.

Miss Meadows *(Aghast)*. Well, Lordy, if dat don't beat all! My suggestion to you is to get yourself home an' in bed, tuck de quilt covers under your chin an' drink plenty of hot tea with molasses . . . cure your Mopes quick as a wink!

(Pause).

What's de Mopes?

Brer Rabbit. Don't know, but I'm headin' off to visit old Aunt Mammy-Bammy . . . She's got de big book jammed full of every ailment dere is an' what's good for its cure.

Miss Meadows. I hope she can cure you fast . . . We have a date for de gatherin' dat Miss Goose is givin' at de old mill pond tonight . . . 'less you've gone an' forgotten already.

Brer Rabbit. Couldn't forget a date with you, Miss Meadows . . . I'll be dere . . . cured an' feelin' fit, if I know Aunt Mammy-Bammy.

(In pain).

Don't you worry none 'bout me, bosom friends . . . I'll be fit as a fiddle in no time . . .

(More pain).

No, don't get close now . . . might be de ketchy kinda Mopes!

(Groans as he exits. Brer Tarrypin chuckles).

Brer Coon. Here comes old Brer Fox and Brer Bear. Dey should be mighty glad to hear de news of Brer Rabbit's ailment.

(Brer Fox and Brer Bear enter exhausted, dragging their clubs and fanning themselves with their hats).

Miss Meadows. Mornin', Brer Fox . . . 'Day to you, Brer Bear . . . the summer mornin' heat got ya down?

(She chuckles).

Brer Coon. I think Brer Rabbit has out-foxed old Brer Fox again . . . dat's what *I* think.

Brer Fox. Well, *I* think you an' that fuzzy-tailed critter is in cahoots! Don't you worry none, dough . . . I'll ketch him . . . he didn't escape us . . . we're hot on de trail right now . . . just takin' a breather before we spring into action. Ain't dat right, Brother Bear?

Brer Bear. Er . . . ah . . . yah . . . right!

Brer Fox. An' when *I* ketch him . . . when *I* do!

Brer Tarrypin. What ya gonna do . . . *if* you ketch him, Brer Fox?

(This question brings Brer Fox back to life. He becomes bug eyed, a maniac. He acts the whole thing out very dramatically).

BRER FOX. Den I'm gonna pull out his moustaches, one by one . . . den two by two! I'll grab him by de scruff of de neck . . . er maybe by de tips of his ear! . . . den swing him around in circles over my head . . . slam him down against de ground . . . an' den when he's so dizzy he's too weak to give me any argument, I'll . . .

(Brer Bear has been taken in with the excitement and now he has his turn, but instead of an imaginary Brer Rabbit, he uses Brer Fox as his victim).

BRER BEAR. . . . I'll womp him on dat fuzzy head!

(Slams Brer Fox with his club).

. . . stomp him!

(Jumps up and down on Brer Fox).

. . . wring his neck!

(Chokes Brer Fox).

. . . twist his foots!

(Brer Fox pounds the ground in pain).

Pick him up an' slap him around!

(Drags Brer Fox to his feet and starts slapping him around. Then suddenly he realizes what he is doing and to whom. His slaps turn to pats and he begins dusting off Brer Fox's clothes. Brer Fox brushes him away, hauls off to kick him).

BRER FOX. You dumb, pea-brained, feather-head!

(Kicks him in the seat).

BRER COON. You're gonna have to work fast den. Cause Brer Rabbit might not be around dese parts very much longer.

BRER FOX. Huh?

BRER BEAR. He said . . .

BRER FOX *(Grabs club away from Brer Bear).* I heard him . . . what do ya mean by dose words?

BRER TARRYPIN. Seems dat Brer Rabbit's come down with a deadly disease an' is plannin' on leavin' de Briar Patch.

BRER FOX. Ya don't mean it!

BRER BEAR. I think he do.

(Brer Fox threatens him with the club).

BRER COON. He's done gone an' caught himself a baaaaaad case of de Mopes!

Brer Fox *(Brer Fox and Brer Bear cling to one another)*. How bad?

Brer Tarrypin and Brer Coon. Real . . . baaaad!

(Brer Bear starts to cry and sniffle. So does Brer Fox until he realizes what this means. Then he hits Brer Bear with the club).

Brer Fox. Whatta ya cryin' for? Dis is our big chance.

(The Villain).

Get him whilst he's weak an' ailin' an' down-trodden . . . come on, let's put our two heads together up on Chikapin Hill and come up with a plan.

(He laughs villainously).

You'll all have to come up an' visit us for a steamin' bowl of rabbit stew!

(He laughs).

Come on, oaf!

(They exit, arguing).

Why I put up with you I'll never know . . . how'd you ever get to be a bear anyhow?

Brer Tarrypin. Old Aunt Mammy-Bammy had best find a cure for Brer Rabbit's Mopes, an' real quick-like, or he'll end up on old Brer Fox's dinner table.

Brer Coon. Dat Brer Rabbit's de cleverest critter around dese parts . . .

Brer Tarrypin. Sure 'nuff is . . . but de Mopes can sure cloud up de quick-thinkin' apparatus.

Miss Meadows. Well, if you two would quit jabberin' about it an' help him out a bit . . . you men critters are all alike . . . a lotta wind . . . with very little movement. I've gotta get over to Miss Goose's an' help her prepare for de gatherin' . . . you keep an eye on Brer Rabbit, now!

(She exits).

Brer Coon. Old Miss Meadows sure has taken a hankerin' to Brer Rabbit . . . I wouldn't be at all surprised if she snagged him for a-comin' fall weddin'.

Brer Tarrypin. Could be . . . could be . . . unless dat old Brer Fox snags him first!

(He laughs).

(Music up as they exit. As soon as they are gone, Brer Fox tip-toes across the back of the set and peers under the bridge. Seeing the coast is clear, he runs off right and appears again with Brer Bear carrying a log with a black glob on it).

Brer Fox (*Snickering the entire time*). We've got him good an' sure dis time . . . hee, hee!

Brer Bear. I'm not sure dat I understands de plan, Brer Fox.

Brer Fox. I wouldn't expect you would . . .

(*He snickers*).

Brer Bear. What's dis here glob of tar on dis old hollow log for?

Brer Fox (*He laughs aloud*). Ewe . . . whee! . . . dat dere's de best part!

(*Laughs again*).

Everytime I think about it, I breaks out with de hysterias.

(*He laughs louder*).

Brer Bear. Well, why don't ya tell me, too, Brer Fox, so dat I can laff, too?

Brer Fox (*He laughs through the entire explanation*). Well, sir, along about any minute now, old Brer Rabbit's gonna come mopin' along down de road . . . sickly an' ailin' an' feelin' without a friend in de world.

(*He rolls on the ground laughing*).

And just 'bout den . . . he spots dis here tar critter on dis here log, mindin' his own bizness . . .

(*Loud laughter as Brer Bear stands scratching his head*).

This here's de best part! . . . Knowin' how dat Brer Rabbit's so friendly an' all with de strangers, he'll shake de hand of de critter made outa tar . . . an' *stick* to him . . . an' den we got him!

(*Hysterical laughter*).

Brer Bear. But we got de glob of tar already!

Brer Fox (*Hitting him with his hat*). Not de tar glob! . . . Brer Rabbit!

Brer Bear. Oho!

(*Deep laugh*).

I gotcha now, Boss . . . but Brer Rabbit ain't no dummy like most . . . He ain't gonna believe dat tar *glob* is supposed to be a tar *critter.*

Brer Fox. Well, I suppose maybe you got somethin' dere . . . but we can fix dat in a jiffy.

(*He pulls two buttons off Brer Bear's coat and sticks them on the tar for eyes*).

Brer Bear. Hey! Dose are my new Sunday-Goin'-To-Meetin' buttons!

BRER FOX. Well, you've got to contribute somethin' . . . Was me who tossled and twirled my head to come up with de whole plan.

(To Brer Bear).

Bend down and pick me up dat stone over dere.

(Brer Bear turns and bends down. When he does Brer Fox pulls a patch of fur out of his seat and plops it on the tar critter's head. Brer Bear stands quickly and runs about fanning his seat with his hat).

BRER BEAR. Hey! What you go an' do a thing like dat for?

BRER FOX. Well, ya ain't never heard of a bald-headed tar-critter before, has ya?

BRER BEAR *(Rubbing his seat).* Well now . . . I think ya really got me dere, Brer Fox.

BRER FOX *(Grabs Brer Bear's hat and plops it on the critter's head: He stands back and admires it).* Something's missing, Brer Bear.

BRER BEAR. Yeah, a piece of my back side.

BRER FOX. Hesh up! He'll be prancin' lippety-clippity down dat road any minute now . . . Gimme dat coat an' don't you gimme no backsass!

(He does and Brer Fox puts it around the Tar Critter's shoulders and laughs).

Dat does it . . . If I didn't know dat was a tar glob, I'd swear it was a real critter.

(Music up).

Quick! Hide behind dis here tree. He's comin' now!

(They hide behind the stage right side of the ramp, in vision behind the poles as Brer Rabbit enters, carrying a carpet bag, up the ramp and over the bridge and down past the log with the tar critter).

BRER RABBIT *(Groaning).* I sure am one ailin' rabbit . . . Old Aunt Mammy-Bammy had best cure dese old Mopes before Brer Fox catches up with me.

(He spots the tar critter and tips his hat as he passes).

Howdy!

(He waits for an answer; when there is none, he takes a step toward it).

Dat dere's either de deafest critter alive or de most unsociablest.

(He yells).

I *says!* Hoooow-dee!

(He waits).

I just can't abide high-falutin' folks.

(He steps right up to it as Brer Fox and Brer Bear snicker).

Where's your politeness? Ain't you gonna say howdy like respectable folks say when dey meet up on de road?

(No answer).

You listen to me, mister . . . I am one ailin' rabbit an' I am declinin' fast . . . but! You friendly up to me an' say howdy back, or else I'll have to wack in your nose! I'll give ya a count of three . . . are ya ready?

(He folds his arms, taps his foot and starts counting).

A one! . . .

(He listens).

A two! . . .

(He waits).

A two an' a half! . . .

(Brer Fox and Brer Bear are rolling on the ground with laughter).

You asked for it, mister . . . ailin' or not ailin' you are down-right, plum unfriendly!

(He rolls up his sleeve, winds up his arm and lets the critter have it right in the nose. His fist sticks).

Hey dere! . . . You best let my fist loose! If you don't let loose of my fist, I'm gonna have to whomp your mouth with my left-over fist!

(He does that and that fist sticks too).

Now dis here has proceeded far enough. You sure are one cranky critter, an' my patience is arguin' with my anger. If you don't let loose of my fists, I'm gonna have to kick you with my behind foots 'til you ain't got no breath left in your body!

(He does and there he is, completely stuck. Brer Fox and Brer Bear come out laughing, aloud).

Brer Fox. We sure ketched you good dis time, Brer Rabbit. You better say your farewell prayers 'cause dis is de very last day of your life!

Brer Bear. You been bouncin' round dis neighborhood for a long time. Now I'm de boss, an' I'm gonna knock your head clean off!

(He lifts his club and is about to hit Brer Rabbit when Brer Fox stops him).

Brer Fox. No, Dat's too easy, an' too quick! We got to make him suffer. I'm gonna fix up a great big fire. Den, when it's good an' hot . . . I'm gonna roast you!

Brer Rabbit *(He has an idea, but acts very scared).* It's just as good dat ya caught me, Brer Fox, 'cause I'm goin' fast with a severe case of de Mopes, an' I'm too weak an' ailin' to fight you back. I don't care what you do with me . . . just so you don't fling me over dere into dat briar patch! Roast me just as hot as you please, but please don't fling me in dat briar patch!

Brer Bear *(Tapping Brer Fox on the shoulder).* Hold on a minute. It's goin' to be a lot of trouble to roast Brer Rabbit. First we'll have to fetch up a pile of kindlin' wood.

Brer Fox. Dat's so . . . well, den, Brer Rabbit . . . I'm goin' to hang you!

Brer Rabbit. Hang me just as high as you please . . . It don't matter in my sickly condition . . . but, please . . . don't fling me in dat briar patch!

Brer Bear. It's goin' to be a lot of trouble to hang Brer Rabbit . . . First, we got to fetch a big, long rope.

Brer Fox. Dat's so . . . well, Brer Rabbit, I expect de best way is to skin you. Come on, Brer Rabbit, let's get started.

Brer Rabbit. Skin me . . . pull out my ears . . . snatch off my legs an' chop off my tail, but . . . please, please,

(Shouts).

please! Don't fling me in dat briar patch!

Brer Bear. Wait a minute, Brer Fox. It ain't goin' to be much fun to skin Brer Rabbit, 'cause he ain't skeered of bein' skinned.

Brer Fox *(Paces, scratching his head).* You sure has got yourself a point dere . . .

(An idea).

But he sure is skeered of dat briar patch . . . An' dat's just where he's goin'! Kerblam! Right in dat briar patch!

(They go to Brer Rabbit and pull him off the tar critter and carry him halfway up the stage right ramp).

You is through sassin' an' bossin' now, Brer Rabbit.

(They swing him back and forth).

A one . . . a two . . . a three, heave ho!

(They toss him over the side of the ramp and wait and listen).

Brer Rabbit. Oaa! . . . oow! ouch! . . . I'm a gonner . . . dis is de end . . . I'm doomed, soon to be a departed rabbit.

(The groans get weaker and weaker as he "dies" very dramatically. Brer Fox and Brer Bear shake hands and pat each other on the back as they cross to the log).

Brer Bear. Dat Brer Rabbit ain't gonna be sassy no more!

Brer Fox. Dis is de end! Brer Rabbit is gone for good!

(From behind the ramp, up pops Brer Rabbit. He scurries to the bridge).

Brer Rabbit. Howdy, Brer Fox and Brer Bear! I told you, an' I told you, not to fling me in dat briar patch. Dat's de one place in all dis world I love de best. De briar patch is de place where I wuz born!

(He laughs).

Brer Fox *(To Brer Bear)*. You lunk head! Why didn't ya think of dat!

(He bops him on the head).

Come on while he's still weak an' ailin'. We'll out run him!

(They rant and rave as they run up the stage right ramp; Brer Rabbit runs down the stage left ramp, grabs his carpet bag, runs up the stage right side across the bridge and off left. Brer Fox and Brer Bear grab the log on their way and follow his path. Weird music, almost electronic, comes up as the pole lights change to blues, reds and greens. Smoke and wind come from behind the bridge as a traveler of flimsy, shredded scrim is drawn across the front of the bridge section. Brer Rabbit can be heard shouting for Aunt Mammy-Bammy in the distance. Brer Tarrypin and the rest appear in fluorescent shredded capes and hoods, moving mysteriously about the stage and waving their arms like spooks. Brer Rabbit enters behind the scrim in a spot and shouts chant-like as the spooks disappear).

Brer Rabbit. Old Aunt Mammy-Bammy, are you here in dis creepy-crawly forest with all de scary spooks an' such? . . . Yoo-hoo . . . Oh, mystified an' mortal fearin' wonder lady of de magical curin' . . . are you at home?

Aunt Mammy *(Her voice amplified from nowhere)*. Dis is de person for whom you is lookin' . . . I am up to my elbow joints with de 'grediants for de Aunt Mammy-Bammy wart removin' liniment an' can't be pestered so . . . go away!

Brer Rabbit. It's me, Aunt Mammy-Bammy, your next of kin nephew who is ailin' an' weakly with de Mopes . . . I come callin' on your magical powers an' purifyin' potions for de qualified cure.

Aunt Mammy. When Aunt Mammy-Bammy says she is busy . . . she is busy! She is goin' to be busy for de next five to three months, so come back next week when she is unfinished bein' busy! . . . now vamoose.

BRER RABBIT. I brung you some fresh rubarb an' freshly picked goobers from my goober patch.

AUNT MAMMY. Huh? . . . Did dat voice dat is so kind an' familiar say dat dey brung goobers an' rubarb?

BRER RABBIT. De juiciest, red, ripe rubarb you ever did see.

AUNT MAMMY. If you leave dose gobblin' goodies dere an' skidaddle . . . de wonder lady of de cure-alls will see you yesterday noon. Now quit pesterin' de genius!

BRER RABBIT (*Coming down in front of the scrim. Performing the greatest death scene ever*). But I need ya now! . . . I am on my last behind foot . . . I feel de wobblies in my knee joints . . . my bones is collapsin' . . . de flutter bugs is settlin' in my head . . . Ugh! . . . ahhhh! Save my last hope for de future!

(*He freezes and starts to shudder all over*).

Dis is it!

(*He yells*).

Ugh! . . . ahhhhh! De wigglies has begun to gain control of my bones . . .

(*He falls to the ground*).

I am a goin' goner . . . Good-bye, wonder lady of de cure alls who has sat back an' watched de last of de livin' kin of hers git kilt by de Mopes . . .

(*He's gone*).

Good . . . bye . . . forever . . . Aunt Mammy . . .!

AUNT MAMMY (*Wailing*). Oohhh! Ahhh! Dey got 'em! Dey got 'em! Don't you move child! Your Aunt Mammy-Bammy is on her way! . . . I'll save you . . .

(*Chants*).

Spirits dat haunt dis poor child's inside sections . . .

(*Yells*).

Hold on a second!

(*Brer Rabbit lifts his head and smiles and winks at the audience; then falls back and groans as Aunt Mammy enters, pushing a book stand on wheels. She is laden down with good luck charms and beads. A stethoscope around her neck, glasses, and smokes a corn cob pipe. She enters wailing and waving her arms and running around Brer Rabbit*).

AUNT MAMMY. Spirits dat mean to carry away dis child . . . scat! Vamoose! An' take de Mopes with you!

(*She waves her charms over him, sprinkling some magic dust*).

Horseshoe . . . clover with de four leaves . . . de bunny foot . . . an' magic up my sleeve . . .

(Brer Rabbit begins to sneeze with all the dust).

Sunny flower an' lizard dust . . .

(She sees he is faking).

Hang it all . . . take 'em if you must!

(Brer Rabbit's eyes open wide).

Brer Rabbit, what do you think you'll achieve by foolin' your aunty . . . You're just makin' believe!

(She laughs hysterically as Brer Rabbit sits upright abruptly).

Ya scamperin' scallywag, is dis another one of your foolin' tricks? Can't fool old Aunt Mammy-Bammy! She can see right through ya!

BRER RABBIT. I shoulda known better den try an' fool *you*, Aunt Mammy . . . I am so weak an' ailin' with de Mopin' dat ole Brer Fox nearly caught me for good dis very mornin'!

AUNT MAMMY. Tch . . . tch . . . tch . . . if dat is so, den you got 'em real baaad! Ain't never seen no one out trick you . . . But dat's what ya get when you messes aroun' with de worries.

BRER RABBIT. Do you have de qualified cure for de Mopes?

AUNT MAMMY. Hee! Hee! Honey, Aunt Mammy-Bammy has got de cure for any kinda ailin' you got . . . Why with de aid of dis official book, I'll have you good as new, lickety-split!

(Flips through the book).

So, de Mopes is what's ailin' you.

(As she flips).

Mopes . . . mopes . . . How do ya spell "mopes"?

BRER RABBIT. You got me, Aunt Mammy-Bammy . . . If I don't know what dey is . . . how could I know how to spell 'em?

AUNT MAMMY. Hmmm . . . you got yourself a point dere.

(She keeps flipping, suddenly:).

Here dey is! . . . Here dey is! De Mopes!

(She reads).

Formerly known as de down-cast dips . . . hmmm . . .

(Mutters as she reads, occasionally tittering. Brer Rabbit tries to read over her shoulder).

Sonny! Dis is de secret book with de magic cures of ten continents . . . kindly stop breathin' down my neck an' set an' wait for de results!

(He moves away).

BRER RABBIT. What does de book say? . . . Is it serious? . . . Will de cure hurt?

AUNT MAMMY. Hush up your mouth . . . How do you 'spect me to read an' listen to your jabberin' all at de same time! I only got two eyes ya know! . . . I got de cure!

(Slams book shut).

An' it is de qualified cure! Stick out your tongue an' say ahh.

(He opens his mouth as she peers in).

Hmmm. hmmm where'd you put your tongue! . . . Oh, dere it is, de little devil, hidin' behin' your molar tooths.

(She puts stethoscope to his heart, but she can't find it).

BRER RABBIT. Do ya hear de Mopes in dere? . . .

(No answer).

Is dey discussin' how dey is gonna take me! . . .

(No answer. . . . He takes the stethoscope and yells in it).

I said . . . Is dey in dere!

(Aunt Mammy's eyes bug out and she screams and falls backwards).

AUNT MAMMY. I ain't deaf! . . . I heard ya! . . . young whippersnapper!

BRER RABBIT. Is dey in dere?

AUNT MAMMY. Oh, dey is in dere all right . . . mopin' aroun' all over de place . . . but I can save ya.

BRER RABBIT. An' I am ready to be saved! . . . Hurry up. What do I have to do?

AUNT MAMMY. Hold on dere . . . dis is gonna take some time . . . ya gotta take it slow an' sneaky-like . . . ya gotta creep up to dose mopes real quiet an' attack 'em whilst dey ain't lookin' . . . I'm gonna need some special 'gredients dat you gotta get me from de outside world.

BRER RABBIT. What do ya need first?

AUNT MAMMY. I needs a handful of de hairs from de turkey buzzard's head.

BRER RABBIT. Dat sounds easy enough. I'll just mosey over to ole Sis Buzzard's nestin' place an' be back before you gobbles up dis sack of goobers.

(He hands sack to her).

Aunt Mammy. Yipee! Gobble up de goobers! Goobers an' rubarb de tastiest combination treat dat I know of! You sure know de way aroun' de back ways to your aunty's heart. Get movin' now before de Mopes changes dere minds an' settles for good.

Brer Rabbit. I'm as good as gone an' come back again.

(He runs up stage right ramp and off left).

Aunt Mammy *(Laughing to herself).* Dat Brer Rabbit will be cured an' gettin' back into de mischief before he even suspects it.

(Laughs).

Dem Mopes an' me, we had a long talk an' we is agreein' on one thing . . . where dere's prankin' an' caperin' about . . . dat Brer Rabbit as sure as shootin' will be smack dab in de middle of it!

(She laughs and then hiccups. She clasps her hand over her mouth).

De hiccy-pup twinges is settlin' in!

(Panic).

De cure!

(She runs to the book, flipping through the pages as she exits, pushing it—mumbling and hiccuping).

(Pole lights return to yellow and orange as wild rock music is heard being played on a very tinny radio. Brer Tarrypin and Brer Coon carry in a bench with a wooden washtub).

Brer Tarrypin. Old Sis Buzzard's sure got de work cut out for her, a nestful of young-uns with more on de way.

Brer Coon. With a nestful of squalkin' buzzards, no wonder she keeps dat rackety radio blarin'.

Brer Tarrypin. Sis is practicin' up for de big dancin' contest try-outs.

(Laughing).

Sis is gettin' to be known as de scrubba-dubba dancin' fool . . . She's comin' now.

(Sis Buzzard enters, a portable radio on a rope hangs from her neck. She carries an armload of clothes, dancing a wild jig the entire time and singing with the music. She wears a bandanna on her head, large thick glasses, apron, etc. You might say Sis Buzzard is truly one ugly girl).

Sis *(Singing and dancing around the stage).* . . . . He wore a black leather jacket an' they called him Ferd . . . But I hankered for him anyways . . . My Ferd de black leather bird . . .

(She spots Brer Tarrypin and Brer Coon, reduces radio volume).

Howdy, Brer Tarrypin . . . Brer Coon . . . What brings you out here to dis neck of de wood?

BRER TARRYPIN. We're checkin' up on Brer Rabbit. Has he been 'round dese here parts today?

SIS (*Laughs*). Just thinkin' 'bout dat scamp makes me convulse with de laffin' jag. I ain't seen him in a monthful of Sundays.

(She laughs).

BRER TARRYPIN. We'd best be moseyin' along . . . de best to de young-uns . . . an' if you ketch sight of Brer Rabbit, tell him we was askin' for him.

SIS. Be happy to oblige ya . . . mosey on by again when you can stay longer.

(They exit as Sis turns up her radio and starts singing and dancing and scrubbing. Brer Rabbit enters up the stage left ramp to the bridge. He stops and stares for a moment at Sis, then he comes down to her).

BRER RABBIT (*With a small wave*). 'Day Sis Buzzard.

(She doesn't hear because of the radio).

'Day Sis Buzzard . . . Howdy!

(Still no response, so he cups his hands to his mouth and shouts).

Howdy!

(Sis screams, throws laundry on his head, knocks him to the ground and starts stomping on him. Then she runs about the stage screeching).

SIS. Buzzard attacker! Help! Nest robber!

BRER RABBIT. Hold on, Sis . . . it's only me, Brer Rabbit.

SIS (*Relieved, she sits on the edge of the bench, fanning herself with her apron, turns off radio*). Land sakes! Mighta knowed it would be you stirrin' up de mischief . . . nearly scared de hair right off de top of my head.

BRER RABBIT (*Crosses to her*). Ya mean it? Maybe I loosened it up a bit dough; maybe it could fall off at any minute.

SIS. You leave my top hairs outa dis. Dey is goin' fast enough as it is without you helpin' dem along.

BRER RABBIT (*Running around the stage*). Maybe you lost some in de scuffle.

SIS (*Laughing*). Land sakes, Brer Rabbit! If you ain't de most laugh-provokin' critter I ever did see! Wish I could sit an' lollygag with ya, but I got to get back to my scrubbin'; tonight's de big Hoot An' Holler Jamboree an' Dancin' Contest.

Brer Rabbit. Are you enterin' dat dancin' contest, too, Sis Buzzard?

Sis. Sure am, an' with de new dance I've been practicin' . . .

(She goes into a few steps).

. . . I am sure to win.

Brer Rabbit. What kinda dance do you call dat?

Sis. An invention of my own . . . "De Sis Buzzard Combination Boogie Woogie Fox Trot Rumba With a Waltz Beat." Don't it really flip your mind?

Brer Rabbit. Not particular . . . but I sure wishes it would flip yours.

Sis. It does, Bunny Man . . . it does! Whoopee!

(She dances).

Brer Rabbit *(Conniving.)* Well, it certainly is peculiar that you should mention it, 'cause I'm enterin' dat dancin' contest, too . . . with a dance invention of my own.

Sis *(Stopping in the middle of a wild movement, stunned).* You are? Why I didn't know dat. What's you callin' *your* dance invention, Brer Rabbit?

Brer Rabbit. It's called "De Hopin' to Git Rid of De Mopin' Stomp With a Bugaloo Beat."

Sis. How does de motions go?

Brer Rabbit. Dey is top secret motions.

Sis. You can trust me, Brer Rabbit. I won't show dem to no one!

Brer Rabbit. I don't know. It took me three an' one half months to invent dose motions.

Sis. I promise! . . . I promise!

Brer Rabbit. It's one of dose dancin' steps dat needs two, an' my partner ain't here.

Sis. Show me what to do . . . I'll do it!

Brer Rabbit. I promised not to reveal my dancin' invention to no one . . . but since you is a friend of de family, I'll show you . . . I'm gonna need some music.

Sis. I'll turn my radio on.

(She does, low volume).

How 'bout Rhupert Racket an de Rollin' Rattlers playin' . . . "Moonshine On De Goober Patch"?

Brer Rabbit. De perfect tune.

Sis. Now what do I do?

BRER RABBIT.   Well, at de beginnin' I just run 'round doin' some jiggy
kinda steppin' . . . den I grabs your hand an' we sashay an' saunter
aroun' a bit.

SIS.   Oh, Brer Rabbit, dat is de bestest dancin' invention I have ever
heard of!

BRER RABBIT.   Now dis is where de excitin' steppin' starts . . . you
grab me by de scruff of de ears an' I grabs you by de top hairs
on de head an' we bops an' hops up an' down in alternatin' motion.

SIS *(Squealing)*.   Oh, Brer Rabbit, dat is de coolest . . . If I do real
good in de practice, maybe I could do it for real with you tonight?

BRER RABBIT.   Oh, I don't know. My partner might be irritable 'bout
it.

SIS.   Let's start de music an' stop de jibberin' . . . an' start de swingin'!

*(She turns up the music and the dance begins as Brer Rabbit
described it. He dances around in the same wild motions, takes
her hand and they do several twirls, etc. Then she grabs his ears
and he grabs the top of her bandanna. She pushes his head down
as he squats: he does the same to her. They do this several times
until Brer Rabbit pushes her down and pulls her head up with a
yank, taking her bandanna and leaving her with a huge bald spot
on her head. Sis squeals and runs about).*

BRER RABBIT.   Sorry, Sis, but dose top hairs more valuable to me now
den dey is valuable to you.

SIS.   You sneaky, connivin' trickin' rattler snake in de tall grass! . . .
I'll chop de fuzzy tail off your hind side!

*(She chases him around the stage and out. All the while, music
is blaring away. As the music fades Miss Meadows and Miss
Goose enter stage right. They cross to stage left as they speak).*

MISS MEADOWS.   I tell you, Miss Goose, I can't seem to snag me dat
fuzzy-eared scallywag.

MISS GOOSE.   Tryin' to ketch dat critter's like tryin' to ketch hold of
a hurrycane's tail.

MISS MEADOWS.   Well, I hope I get him before dat ole Brer Fox does,
'specially in his serious mopin' condition.

MISS GOOSE.   You don't see any rain seeds floatin' around in de sky,
do you? Hate to have de gatherin' spoiled with a lotta overcast.

MISS MEADOWS.   Fine, clear, sunny-shiney summer day.

MISS GOOSE *(At washtub)*.   I'd better get de Monday mornin' washin'
strung on de line before de rain seeds changes dere minds.

(She bends over the tub and drops her glasses in).

My gosh an' my goodness, I dropped my eye spectacles into de
washin' water!

(She fishes her hand in and tries to find them. Brer Fox appears behind them on the ramp and hides behind the bridge rail watching).

I can't see no one, nor no thing without my eye spectacles. Miss Meadows, would you run over to de house an' fetch my extra pair off de mantle piece?

MISS MEADOWS. You keep fishin' in dat tub for dem . . . I'll fetch de other pair.

(She hurries off. Miss Goose keeps fishing while Brer Fox tiptoes down the ramp. He crosses stage right and speaks to the audience).

BRER FOX. Since ole Brer Rabbit has slipped through my fingers along with my rabbit stew . . . I'll have to settle for a roasted goose dinner instead.

(He changes his voice).

Yoo hoo, Miss Goose. I can't find your eye spectacles anywheres.

MISS GOOSE *(Squinting to see)*. Well, if dat don't bang my times! Dey was dere dis mornin' earlier . . . come lead me into dat house. Maybe I can search 'em up.

BRER FOX *(Producing a large sack, he speaks to the audience)*. I got dis day's supper in de bag.

(He titters as he crosses to her, ready to plop the bag over her head).

MISS MEADOWS *(From off stage)*. I fetched 'em, Miss Goose.

(Brer Fox's eyes bug out).

BRER FOX. I've got to hide!

(He puts the sack over his head and squats on the ground as Miss Meadows enters).

MISS MEADOWS. Dey was right where you said dey was.

(She sees the sack).

Miss Goose, how'd you move dis heavy sack of laundry by yourself?

(Brer Rabbit comes rushing over the bridge and crosses to Miss Meadows).

BRER RABBIT. Howdy again, Miss Meadows.

(Brer Fox's head peers from under the sack towards us with a bewildered look on his face).

MISS MEADOWS. What you doin' out an' scamperin' around . . . sickly as you are.

Livin' de Life, as produced by Pickwick Players, of Midland, Texas

BRER RABBIT. Gatherin' de 'gredients for Aunt Mammy-Bammy's curin' potion.

(Crosses to sack and sits. Brer Fox groans).

You sure got yourself a sack full of de groany kinda laundry, Miss Goose.

MISS GOOSE.   I wish I could see who was talkin' at me.

MISS MEADOWS.   Here is your eye spectacles, Miss Goose.

(She hands them to her).

MISS GOOSE.   Ah, much better.

(She steps back).

My stars an' crowns! Brer Rabbit, what are you doin' here abouts? . . .

(Sis Buzzard is heard squealing and screeching off stage).

BRER RABBIT.   Sorry I can't stay longer an' pass de time of day with you, but I gotta get dis potion material to Aunt Mammy-Bammy quick-like.

(He runs off as Miss Meadows turns to Miss Goose. As they speak, the laundry sack slowly moves stage right).

MISS GOOSE.   Ain't dat ole Sis Buzzard a 'squealin' an' squalkin' dis way?

(Sis enters carrying a club. She is really winded).

SIS.   Has you ladies spied dat floppy-eared connivin' critter, Brer Rabbit?

MISS MEADOWS.   What has dat critter up an' done now?

SIS.   Dat critter has done connived me outa de top center hairy section of my head . . . dat's what!

(The ladies are aghast. Sis paces back and forth between the ladies and the sack).

An' when I gets my hands on him, I'm gonna whomp him with dis here club . . .

(She hits the sack).

Den I'm gonna kick him in de shins!

(She kicks the bag. Brer Fox groans and peers out from the bottom).

An' I just might whomp him again!

(She does).

An' kick him again!

(She does).

BRER FOX *(Stands and throws off the sack).* I've had it! Have mercy on a poor bruised up critter!

(On his knees).

MISS MEADOWS. Brer Fox, you sneaky snake in de grass!

MISS GOOSE. He was stalkin' me for de dinner plate, I know it!

(She grabs a stick and goes after him. Miss Meadows does the same).

BRER FOX. Now hold on a minute, ladies, you got it all wrong . . . I was . . .

SIS. I know what you was after. You're just as bad as dat Brer Rabbit, pickin' on defenseless lady folk!

(They start chasing him up one ramp and down the other and finally off. Brer Rabbit, who has been hiding behind the bridge, pops out laughing).

BRER RABBIT. Brer Fox is gonna be kept mighty busy for de time bein' . . . long enough for me to get cured of de Mopes . . . I hopes.

(He exits yelling).

Aunt Mammy-Bammy! I got de 'gredients . . . Can you hear me yellin' at ya?

(Brer Coon and Brer Tarrypin enter over the bridge).

BRER COON. Dat Brer Rabbit must really got de Mopes bad . . . ain't seen nor heard a peep outa him all mornin'.

BRER TARRYPIN. Sure is one of de quietest, most peacefullest days I can recall.

(They cross to the bench and tub and carry them out as they go).

BRER COON. How's about us goin' up to de mill pond for a little fishin' . . . more excitement up dere den aroun' here.

BRER TARRYPIN. Good idea . . . take advantage of de peace an' de solitude.

(They exit. As the lights cross-fade to the blues and greens, the weird music comes up. Brer Rabbit enters in a spot).

BRER RABBIT. Aunt Mammy-Bammy! I'm back fast as I promised . . . Can you hear me?

(He yells).

Can . . . you . . . hear . . . me!

AUNT MAMMY *(Enters in a wheel chair).* Land sakes . . . I ain't deef! Whataya want dis time!

(Groan).

Oh, I got de ailin's!

BRER RABBIT. You said you had de cure.

AUNT MAMMY. Dis is a new foreign kinda ailin' . . . dere ain't no cure in de book.

BRER RABBIT. Are ya ailin' bad?

AUNT MAMMY. De baddest ailin' I ever had de fortune of comin' across . . . a combination of de rubarb rub-a-dubs an' de hysterical hiccy-pup twinges . . .

(She hiccups).

. . . with a slight toothache.

(Groan).

BRER RABBIT. Have ya tried hot tea an' molasses?

AUNT MAMMY. Dat's how I got de toothache.

BRER RABBIT. Well, I warned you about eatin' all dat rubarb an' goobers at one time. What's de last 'gredient for de Mope curin' potion, Aunt Mammy?

AUNT MAMMY. De ailin' has clogged my thinkin' apparatus . . . I don't remember.

BRER RABBIT. Look in de magic book, Aunt Mammy . . . dis is a matter of life . . . or rabbit stew for me!

AUNT MAMMY. I remember somethin' about *(Hiccups)* a beat-up bee hive dat's been vacated of de bees in some cure potion of late.

BRER RABBIT. Dat must be it! I'll be back in no time with de 'gredient . . . on my way I'll stop an' see Doc Crow an' send him over to take a look at your ailin's.

(Exit).

AUNT MAMMY. I don't want dat quack in dis vacinity!

(Hiccups and groans).

Oh, no . . . look out, ailin' bones an' twitterin' tummy, de door flew open an' here come de vibratin' vapors!

(She groans and exits as quiet, peaceful music mixed with birds chirping, etc. comes up with the cross-fading of the lights to sunshine. Brer Tarrypin and Brer Coon enter with fishing poles up the up right ramp. Brer Bear comes up the other side).

BRER BEAR. Hey dere, fellas. You ain't seen de sights of Brer Fox, has you?

BRER COON. Not since dis mornin', Brer Bear.

Brer Tarrypin. Maybe he caught him de Mopes from Brer Rabbit an' is home in de bed ailin'!

(Laughs).

Brer Coon. Step alive, Brer Tarrypin, before de fishes stop de bitin' for de day.

(They exit as Brer Bear stands scratching his head. From under the bridge Brer Fox's head appears).

Brer Fox. Psst!

(Brer Bear looks around).

Pssst!

(Brer Bear looks again).

Down here, lughead!

Brer Bear *(Looks down).* What are you doin' down dere, Brer Fox?

Brer Fox. I'm hidin'.

Brer Bear. Hidin' from what, Brer Fox?

Brer Fox. Hidin' from de Gully Wampers!

Brer Bear. What did de gully wampers ever do to you, Brer Fox?

Brer Fox. Never you mind! . . . Git down here! We got to discover a new plan . . .

(Brer Bear crosses under the bridge).

De time is runnin' out . . . We got to nab dat Brer Rabbit *today!*

(From off stage we hear Brer Rabbit entering).

Ssh! I hear dat slippery scoundral now.

(Brer Rabbit enters and crosses to the bridge, directly above Brer Fox and Brer Bear. A crow caws).

Brer Rabbit *(Shouting up).* 'Day to you, Dr. Crow . . . you're just de bird I'm lookin' for. Ole Aunt Mammy-Bammy is ailin' real bad with de achin' an' de painin'. Could you kinda fly by over an' take a look in on her?

Doc Crow *(Voice only).* Hee, hee! Never thought I'd live to see de day dat ole Aunt Mammy-Bammy would need de aid of me.

(Laughs).

Gonna be passin' over dat way later in de mornin' . . . Would take great pleasure in landin' at her place!

Brer Rabbit. Thanks, Doc Crow . . . but, hurry!

(Caws fading in the distance).

See you at de gatherin' later in de day . . .

(He yawns. To himself).

All dis helter-skelter runnin' aroun' has brung de sleepiness to my
eyes . . . *(Yawns)* . . . I hope de sleepies ain't connivin' with de
Mopes to get me. *(Yawns)* . . . De sun's still hangin' high in de
sky . . . maybe I got time for forty winks before I proceeds.

*(He sits on the bridge, leaning against a post, and as he speaks
his voice weakens and he falls asleep).*

. . . Ole Brer Fox is probly in de next county by dis time any how
. . . ain't no worries 'bout him . . . least ways *dis* day . . .

*(He's asleep, snoring. Brer Fox and Brer Bear have come out of
hiding).*

BRER FOX.   We got him for good dis time . . . Look at him just a settin'
an' a waitin' to be stewed.

(Snickers). (To Brer Bear).

Now you sneak up de back side an' I'll sneak up de front side
. . . When I count three you clonk him on de head and tie him up
. . . You got de rope?

BRER BEAR.   I sure do, Boss!

BRER FOX.   Good . . . let's hurry an' move in . . . quiet-like now . . .

*(They do. Brer Fox tip-toes over to the bottom of the stage left
ramp. Brer Bear follows, only he gets his feet all tangled in the
rope and falls into Brer Fox. Brer Fox turns and tries to hush
him up. Brer Bear gathers himself together and they proceed,
except Brer Bear trips on the edge of the ramp and falls).*

BRER FOX.   You're gonna ruin de bestest chance we ever had, I just
know it!

*(They proceed as planned. Brer Fox is upstage of Brer Rabbit.
Brer Bear above his head. Brer Bear raises his club to clonk
Brer Rabbit on the head just as Brer Fox bends down to look
closer and he gets him instead. Brer Fox raises up and dizzily
swirls around nearly falling off the bridge. Brer Rabbit just keeps
snoring as Brer Bear ties him up).*

BRER BEAR.   I got him tied up, Boss, real tight an' cozy.

BRER FOX.   Huh? Oh, yeah, good.

(He wakes up).

Ya mean we got him? . . . I mean we really got him! Yahoo!

(Brer Rabbit wakes up).

Oh, we gotcha now, Brer Rabbit, an' dere ain't no way you're
gonna get away dis time.

Brer Rabbit. Well, now, you sure do, don't ya!

(He laughs).

You sure do!

(Brer Fox puts a noose around Brer Rabbit's neck).

Brer Fox. An' we're gonna roast ya . . . roast ya for our dinner!

(Brer Rabbit laughs).

Maybe you didn't hear me, Brer Rabbit. I said . . . we're gonna *roast* ya.

(Brer Rabbit laughs louder).

Brer Bear. I guess you don't understand . . . Brer Fox says, we are goin' to *roast ya on a burnin' fire!* Now dat's no laughin' matter. You should be skeered!

Brer Rabbit. Oh, I heard you, Brer Fox.

(He laughs).

Brer Fox. Den why you laffin'?

Brer Rabbit. I just can't control myself . . . 'cause I've just come from my laffin' place.

(He laughs again).

Brer Bear *(Scratching his head).* Laffin' place? What's a laffin' place?

Brer Rabbit. It's a kinda secret place dat only I knows about.

Brer Fox. A secret kinda place? Hmmm . . . Brer Rabbit, tell me some more about dis laffin' place of yours . . . an' I don't wanta hear no sassy kinda talk outa you! Tell me now an' I mean it!

Brer Rabbit *(Laughs throughout).* Oh, it's not de kinda place dat you can talk about . . . I has to show it to you. An' since I'm all roped up here I can't very well do dat now, can I?

(He laughs more, rolling all over the place, Brer Fox and Brer Bear watch in astonishment).

Brer Fox. Come on over here, Brer Bear . . . We gotta do some plannin'.

(They come downstage and Brer Rabbit just keeps laughing).

Now I gotta know about dis laffin place an' I gotta know now! What do you think?

Brer Bear. Oh, I agrees . . . I always agrees.

Brer Fox. Well, dis is what we're gonna do . . .

(They huddle and whisper. Brer Rabbit stops laughing and tries to hear. They stop and look up quickly when they hear he has

stopped laughing. He goes back to laughing and they move farther away, then . . .).

Brer Rabbit, we'll make you a fair an' square deal.

(He crosses to him).

We want you to take us to dat secret laffin' place right here an' now . . . *den* we'll come back an' roast you. Now dat's de fairest kinda deal I can offer at dis time . . . do you agree?

BRER RABBIT. Dat sounds like a mighty fair an' square deal to me, Brer Fox.

BRER FOX *(Takes the end of the rope).* Den rise up an' get a movin'.

BRER RABBIT *(Laughing).* I gets to laffin' just thinkin' 'bout dat secret place!

BRER BEAR. If you ask me he's got a bad case of de laffin' sickness, double combined with de mopin' Mopes.

BRER FOX *(Slaps him with his hat).* Well, nobody did any askin'. Come on, Brer Rabbit, lead de way.

(They cross the bridge to stage right down the stage right ramp across the stage and out downstage left. Brer Tarrypin and Brer Coon enter down stage right. Miss Meadows enters up left to the bridge).

MISS MEADOWS. Well, where have you two been hidin' out with all de commotion of dis day . . . You men folks never seems to be aroun' when you're needed.

BRER TARRYPIN. Commotion! Why dis has been de quietest . . . uncomotionest day dis place has ever seen, what with Brer Rabbit down with de Mopes an' all.

MISS MEADOWS. Just shows how much you two know! De trouble an' de mischief has been lurkin' 'round every bend today and what you two doin? Fishin'! Land sakes, does de trouble need to whomp you on de head before you knows you're in it?

BRER COON. You're talkin' round in de riddles today, Miss Meadows . . . explain yourself.

MISS MEADOWS. Well, you just mosey over to Miss Goose with me an' between de both of us de story will be told.

(They exit with Miss Meadows stage left as Brer Rabbit and the other two enter stage right under the bridge).

BRER RABBIT *(Laughing).* Well, dis here is de place.

BRER FOX *(Winded, looking around).* Why dis is de very same place we started out from over an hour ago! Is dis another one of dose famous prankin' tricks of yours . . . 'cause if it is . . .!

Brer Rabbit. Dis is no prankin' trick, Brer Fox.

(He laughs).

I told ya it was a secret place, an' unless I took ya aroun' in circles an' confused ya a little, you'd know where it was . . . den it wouldn't be a secret no more.

Brer Bear. Well, how come I'm not laffin' den, if dis here is dat laffin' place of yours?

Brer Fox. Yeah! How come dat is . . . huh? I don't see nothin' to laugh at.

Brer Bear. Or me! . . . I don't even *feel* funny!

Brer Rabbit. Oh, you will . . . you just step up behind dem bushys over dere.

Brer Fox. Is dat where de secret hidin' place is hidin'? Come on, Brer Bear, let's go an' have a look.

Brer Bear. I'm beginnin' to chuckle a little bit already.

(They go behind the bushes. Brer Rabbit takes off the rope and rushes to the tree).

Brer Fox *(His head above the bush).* I still ain't doin' no laffin'! Are you sure dis ain't another one of your prankin' tricks?

Brer Rabbit. Certainly not! You just pop back down dere behind dat bushy an' wait! . . . de laffin' will start any minute now.

(Brer Fox goes back behind the bush. Brer Rabbit takes a stick and loosens the beehive from the tree. It falls behind the bush. Brer Fox and Brer Bear run out from behind the bushes yelling and screaming. Brer Bear has the hive on his head. They run all over the stage—up ramps and down—swatting bees all the way. Brer Bear finally gets the hive off his head and tosses it behind the bush. They end their running on the bridge. When the bees are gone, Brer Rabbit comes out from behind the bush carrying the hive and laughing madly).

Brer Bear. Looky dere . . . dat connivin' rabbit had dis scheme planned all de time!

Brer Fox. Why, you slinkin' low-down watchermacollum! You said dis was a laffin' place!

Brer Rabbit. I said dis was *my* laffin' place . . .

(He laughs).

An' dis is de best laff I've ever had!

(He laughs louder. Every other creature in the forest laughs, too).

Thanks for clearin' de bees outa de hive for me, too.

(He laughs as he scampers off).

BRER FOX. Dagnabbit! I think we has been tricked again!

(*He slams his hat on the ground*).

If all you critters don't stop laffin' dat laffin' noise right now, I'll
. . . I'll . . .

BRER BEAR. You'll what, Brer Fox?

BRER FOX. I'll . . . Hey! You up dere! Are you laffin' at me? Cause
if you are . . .!

DOC CROW (*Voice only*). Why, Brer Fox, you mean to say you ain't
got *yourself* a laffin' place?

BRER FOX. Where can I get me one of dose laffin' places . . . I needs
me one bad!

DOC CROW. Everybody needs themselves a laffin' place . . . an' trouble
is most folks don't take time out to go lookin' for one.

BRER BEAR. Where do you find 'em?

DOC CROW. Nobody can tell you where to find it . . . Where it is for
one person ain't de same for another . . . but when you find it

(*He laughs*).

you keep goin' back to it, 'cause it is de happiest place aroun'!

(*He laughs, followed by the rest of the forest*).

BRER FOX. Bah! Who needs one anyways . . .

(*To the trees*).

Ah, you're all a bunch of laffin' fools! Come on, Brer Bear, let's
get away from dis fool place!

(*They exit as the hysterical laughter fades into the wierd music
of Aunt Mammy-Bammy's forest. The pole lights fade and the
ragged scrim is pulled across*).

BRER RABBIT. Ole Aunt Mammy-Bammy, it's me again, come back
with de second 'gredient for de Mope curin' potion . . . Can you
hear me . . .? Yoo hoo . . . I said . . .

AUNT MAMMY (*Entering with a huge ice bag on her head*). I hear ya!
What do you think I am, deaf! Ya loud-mouthin' babblin' fool!
Why don't ya quit buggin' me! Oh, my head . . .!

(*She hiccups*).

Ohhh!

BRER RABBIT. You should of seen me, Aunt Mammy-Bammy!

(*He laughs*).

I tricked ole Brer Fox an' Brer Bear dis time worser den de last!

(*Laughs*).

An' ole Sis Buzzard . . .

(Laughs).

You should of seen it . . . I really had to use my wits to get dat first 'gredient. It's turnin' out to be de most funnest day I has had in years!

Aunt Mammy. Den what's your problem den?

Brer Rabbit. All de time it's worryin' . . . worryin' . . . whether or not I'll get myself caught . . . den worryin' when I don't . . . dere's too many worryin's, Aunt Mammy.

Aunt Mammy. I don't understand you folks . . . ya worries when ya got de troubles . . . an' den ya worries when ya don't. Why do ya think I hides myself out here in de wood . . . to hide from all you worriers!

Brer Rabbit. Maybe I should do dat, too . . . I got it! I'll move into de wood with you for a spell.

Aunt Mammy. Oh, no you don't! You are one problem I don't need!

Brer Rabbit. Den what should I do . . .? Let de Mopes take me away for good, or wait for Brer Fox to do it? Dis is a worryin' problem.

Aunt Mammy. If you an' dat whole lot of critters out dere would just quit de feudin' an' worryin' over de troubles an' start livin' de life, you'd find you ain't got no troubles at all!

Brer Rabbit. You mean call a halt to de prankin' an' caperin'?

Aunt Mammy. Dat might just be de thing dat's been causin' all de worryin' to begin with.

Brer Rabbit. You say if I stops de trick playin', dat will stop de worryin'? An' de Mopin' will go away?

Aunt Mammy. Might be de solid cure for de whole lot of ya.

Brer Rabbit. I'll make de 'nouncement tonight at de gatherin' meetin' . . . from now on, all de prankin' an' caperin' is stoppin' in order to save de worryin' . . . I has spoken! Do you got a temporary cure for de Mopes dat will last till I call a halt at de gatherin'?

Aunt Mammy. If you ain't de pesterin'est critter I ever laid eyes on . . . Gimme dose 'gredients you got!

(He gives them to her).

Now go get me dat mashin' up bowl an' de spices an' stuff over dere.

(He runs over and pulls a small unit with mixing bowl and spice rack on stage).

Now I puts dese in de bowl an' adds de Aunt Mammy-Bammy secret stuff . . .

(Weird music as she goes through her spell).

I adds a handful of warts an' de tongue of de lizard . . . A rattle or two from de rattly snake's tail an' de left middle section of de porky pine's gizzard . . .

(She cackles).

Now for de fun part . . . a pinchy of dried up snow . . . from last year's blizzard . . .

(She tosses it in the pot—A puff of smoke. She cackles).

It's done! It's done!

(She puts a ladle full in a large bug sprayer).

Now stand over dere—I has to spray you all over with dis potion an' let loose with some more of de magical words.

(Weird music again as she sprays, hopping around chanting).

I am talkin' to you . . . oh, Mopies dat live in de deep . . . skoot an' skidaddle for de time bein' . . . an' sleep . . . I'm sprayin' dis child an' I don't want to hear a peep! Rooty begger . . . turnip greens . . . cabbages an' spinaches . . . You Mopes stay ,asleep an' be gone with de itches!

(She cackles with delight).

Any minute now Brer Rabbit, de itchin' will begin.

(Cackles).

and when it does . . .

BRER RABBIT. What will happen when de itchin' starts, Aunt Mammy?

AUNT MAMMY. De itchin' is de first cousin twice removed of de mopes, and dey is feudin' folk indeed . . . *(Cackles)* . . . lordy, when dose two gets together dey really causes de commotions.

BRER RABBIT. You means de itchin' and de mopin' is gonna fight it out in my innards.

AUNT MAMMY *(Cackles).* Yes sir, when dat itchin' begins dere is gonna be a commotion goin' on in dose innards of yours de likes of which you has never seen. When de itchin' goes away . . . *(Cackles)* . . . de mopes will go with 'em and you will be cured.

BRER RABBIT. I'm mighty grateful to you Aunt Mammy . . . I see dat *your* ailin' has gone, too.

AUNT MAMMY. Huh? Oh, yeah. So it has! *(Cackles)* . . . Couldn't help but taste dose 'gredients as I mixed up de batch.

(Dawns on her).

I has found another cure for de book! . . . Do you remember what I put in dat stuff? . . . Dagnabbit, dat's what I get for experimentin' with foreign 'gredients!

BRER RABBIT. I got to be hurryin', Aunt Mammy-Bammy. Will ya be joinin' us at de gatherin'?

AUNT MAMMY. I usually don't partake of de festivities . . . but I wouldn't miss dis one for de world!

BRER RABBIT *(As he exits)*. I'm grateful for de advices an' de secret to de permanent cure . . . Dere will be no more prankin' an' caperin' out of dis rabbit no more!

AUNT MAMMY *(Chuckling)*. Don't speak out de words you're gonna have to eat later . . . I'll teach dat young scallywag!

(Laughs).

Dat potion kinda worked de wonders . . . cured my rubarbs, my hiccy-pups, an' dat fool rabbit's pesterin'.

(Really laughs).

Dat potion with de itchin' powder is de bestest idea I has ever had!

(She cackles).

Wonder what it was dat I sampled an' cured my ailin'? Was it de honey . . .

(She tastes it).

Or was it de rooty begger combined with de rubarb . . . I know, I'll start over from de beginnin' . . . What do I need . . . one sack of fresh goobers an' a bunch of red, ripe rhubarb. Look out tummy, de hiccy-pup twinges is returnin' again to visit.

(She cackles and pushes the table out as she exits. The lighting remains the same except for one pole light which is white and shining at the foot of the bridge—the moon).

(Miss Goose and Miss Meadows enter jabbering and set two sections of cattails and reeds in a half circle around the base of the bridge—the pond. They also carry picnic baskets).

MISS GOOSE. Even de moon has come out for de gatherin'.

MISS MEADOWS. I hope dat pesky rabbit is over de mopin' sickness.

MISS GOOSE. You said you weren't gonna speak to dat scoundrel.

MISS MEADOWS. I ain't an' dat's final!

(Brer Tarrypin and Brer Coon enters).

MISS MEADOWS. Speakin' of not speakin' . . . here come dose other two I ain't speakin' to.

Miss Goose. Sure is gonna be one quiet gatherin' . . . what with nobody speakin' to no one. Here comes Sis Buzzard.

(Sis enters, all gussied up wearing a wild wig with sausage curls and excited as she can be).

Sis. I won! I won! I won de jackpot!

(The girls gather around Sis congratulating her).

Thanks to Brer Rabbit.

Miss Meadows. What did de scamp do to you dis time?

Sis. Well, I figured since he stole my top hair piece dat I'd steal his dancin' invention . . . an' I won de jackpot with his very own invention!

Miss Goose. What did ya win?

Sis. A year's supply of clothespins, a certificate for six free dancin' lessons an' dis brand new top head of hair!

(The girls squeal with excitement).

Brer Tarrypin *(Who has been sitting on the edge of the ramp smoking his pipe).* Just goes to show ya dat Brer Rabbit's prankin' an' caperin' don't always have de bad results.

Brer Coon. An' speakin' of de devil . . . here he comes now.

(Brer Rabbit enters to the bridge and stops short when he sees Sis Buzzard).

Brer Rabbit. Evenin' all . . . mighty nice night for a gatherin' . . . what with de moon out an' all.

Sis. You like my new head of hair, Brer Rabbit? I won it at de Hoot An' Holler Jamboree an' Dancin' Contest . . . with de "Hopin' To Get Rid of De Mopin' Stomp."

Brer Rabbit. Why, you look like a new buzzard, hardly recognized you . . . thought you was a motion picture actress.

Sis *(Embarrassed).* Ah, Brer Rabbit . . . you sure do lay on de flatteries.

Brer Tarrypin. When we gonna eat?

Miss Meadows. Mighta known you'd get to de food question sooner or later.

Miss Goose. Shouldn't we wait for Brer Fox an' de others?

Brer Tarrypin. I wouldn't count too heavy on Brer Fox an' Brer Bear showin' dere faces at dis gatherin'.

Brer Coon. Dey's afraid de ladies will whomp de daylights outa dem.

Miss Meadows. You hush up or I'll whomp de nighttimes outa you!

Brer Rabbit.   If an' when you are through arguin' I have a important world-changin' announcement to announce.

(Everyone babbles).

Brer Coon.   What's dis world-changin' announcement all about, Brer Rabbit?

Brer Rabbit.   Well, now you settle yourselves down an' I'll tell ya.

(They do).

It seems dat 'cause of all de prankin' an' caperin' dere's been 'mongst us all an awful lot of quarrelin' an' worryin'. An' de quarrelin' an' worryin' is causin' an awful lot of mopin'.

(The itching starts. Brer Rabbit stands stiff and bug-eyed and starts to squirm).

An' de itchin' . . . I mean de mopin' . . . is itchin' . . . I mean, causin'

(He yells).

Aunt Mammy-Bammy, wherever you are . . . dey is here an' dey is startin' to argue with each other!

Miss Meadows.   What's de matter with you, Brer Rabbit?

Brer Rabbit *(Squirming).* Its . . . why . . . er . . . ah . . . it's nothing.

(He leans against a tree and rubs his back. Aunt Mammy-Bammy enters and watches and laughs, unnoticed from the sidelines).

But it occurred to me while I was itchin' . . . layin'! in de sick bed dat . . .

(During this scene Brer Rabbit is hopping, rolling, and squirming all over the stage. The movement should never stop as he itches, rubs and speaks all at the same time).

. . . Dat all de time us critters is quarrelin' an' worryin' over de troubles dat we wouldn't have in de first place if we didn't quarrel an' worry . . . dat we should call us a truce an' stop all de itchin' . . . troublin'! . . . an' worryin' an' start livin' de life instead!

(Everyone mumbles in agreement).

Miss Meadows.   You mean you're puttin' an end to all your prankin' an' caperin'?

Brer Rabbit.   Dat's right, Miss Meadows . . . 'stead of prankin' dere will be workin' . . . 'stead of caperin' dere will be itchin' . . . I mean fishin'!

Miss Meadows.   Dat sure is a world-changin' announcement, all right, Brer Rabbit. An' de wisest announcement dat's been announced in dese parts in many a fool moon . . . Are you sure you're all right, Brer Rabbit?

Brer Rabbit. Fine . . . mighty fine.

Miss Meadows. Well, now dat dat's settled let's everyone have some good food an' celebrate de new Brer Rabbit.

(Brer Rabbit is hanging from the bridge up-side down trying to scratch the bottom of his feet. As he lifts his foot, he falls from the bridge into the pond. Everyone rushes to the pond. Aunt Mammy crosses to the bridge laughing).

Miss Goose. Aunt Mammy-Bammy! As I live an' breath! What brings you out of de creepy crawly forest? . . . I thought you was in hidin' forever an' a day!

Aunt Mammy. Well, de forever is over an' dis is de day I wouldn't of missed for all de cure pills in de world.

(She laughs).

Brer Rabbit *(He pops up from behind the reeds and sees Aunt Mammy).* Aunt Mammy-Bammy, de curin' potion has worked! De itchin' is gone an' so is de mopin'.

(Everyone cheers).

Let's gather 'round de fire an' dig into de food!

(They all do as Brer Fox and Brer Bear appear behind the stage left trees).

Aunt Mammy. Did you say food?

Sis. I sure am gonna miss de old Brer Rabbit.

(She laughs).

Just thinkin' 'bout de trickin' you has finagled . . .

(She laughs).

makes me laff.

Miss Meadows. Well, I'm gonna enjoy de new Brer Rabbit.

Aunt Mammy. An' I'm just sittin' an' waitin'.

Brer Rabbit. Sittin' an' waitin' for what, Aunt Mammy-Bammy?

Aunt Mammy. For de *final* results.

(She laughs. Brer Fox and Brer Bear make a noise. Brer Rabbit's ears perk up).

Brer Rabbit. Who's dere?

Brer Tarrypin. Ain't nobody . . . only de fireflies lightin' up dere fires.

Brer Rabbit. Hush up!

Brer Coon. Maybe it's de night owl shakin' de day off his fedders.

(As Brer Fox and Brer Bear tip-toe from one tree to another).

Brer Rabbit. Sshhh . . . it's dose varmits Brer Fox an' Brer Bear, sure as you live dey're plannin' how to nab some of dis food for dere dinner. Hide dose picnic lunches quick-like.

(They set them behind the trees. The ladies huddle together, frightened).

Brer Rabbit *(In a whisper).* Dey is lurkin' over dere in de bushys . . . You just leave dem to me an' do what I says.

(He winks, then speaks loudly. Aunt Mammy just keeps eating and watching and chuckling).

Dis here fire must be 'bout hot enough, don't you think, Brer Tarrypin? . . . 'cause we got a real feast to cook tonight. How are we ever gonna eat such a smashin' dinner . . . just seven of us . . . what a pity we don't have more at de gatherin' . . . dere's enough here for two more . . .

(There is a commotion and out walks Brer Fox and Brer Bear).

Well, bang my times, if it ain't Brer Fox an' Brer Bear! Come on over to de fire! We sure is glad to see ya! Why we was just discussin' dis minute how we was goin' to eat all dis food by ourselves . . . wasn't we now?

(Everyone mumbles yes).

Brer Fox. I don't see no food.

Brer Bear. Me neither.

Brer Rabbit. Course you don't see any food now . . . but just you wait.

Brer Fox. Where is dis food anyhows?

Brer Rabbit. Why, right over dere in de ole mill pond. But ssh!

(Whispers).

It's waitin' dere dis very minute . . . de finest mess of fishes in de world!

Brer Bear. What kinda fishes?

Brer Rabbit. De fattest, juiciest, most tastiest fishes you ever laid your eyes on.

Brer Fox. Hummph! An' just how you gonna ketch 'em?

(Stands close to Brer Rabbit).

Ole Aunt Mammy-Bammy gonna use some of dat magic of hers?

Aunt Mammy. Just might be . . . ya long-nosed fuzzy-headed scally-waggin' varmint.

(She lets loose some wailing and Brer Fox jumps into Brer Bear's arms).

BRER RABBIT. Sssh! Dese ain't no ordinary sorta fishes . . . on nights like dese when de moon's up in de sky, dese fishes come right to de top of de water. All you have to do is reach down an' snatch dem up!

BRER FOX *(Taken in)*. You don't say!

BRER RABBIT. Come on! It's gettin' late an' I'm gettin' hungry! You ladies stay here an' jostle de fire.

(Brer Fox, Brer Bear and Brer Rabbit cross to the bridge).

Oh dear! . . . Oh my! . . . tch . . . tch . . . tch!

BRER FOX. What's de matter, Brer Rabbit?

BRER RABBIT. Dis is awful bad . . . awful bad! But de bad luck's got to come some time an' it sure has come tonight! De moon has fallen into de pond an' is layin' on top of all dose fishes!

BRER FOX. Sure enough! . . . Dere's de moon down dere layin' on top of dose fishes.

BRER BEAR. I don't see no fishes.

BRER FOX. What's wrong with you? What's wrong with dose eyes of yours . . . see 'em?

BRER BEAR. Oh, now I see 'em . . . now I see 'em!

BRER RABBIT. De way I see it is dis way. Less we get dat moon out of dis pond . . . we ain't gonna have no fishes for de gatherin' dinner.

BRER FOX. An' how we goin' to git dat moon out of de pond?

BRER RABBIT. How? . . . Well, I expect de best way is to get us a fishin' net. With dat, we'll drag de moon outa de water in no time flat.

BRER TARRYPIN. You can borrow mine, Brer Rabbit.

BRER RABBIT. Good . . . an' since I can run faster den you, I'll go fetch it . . . You ladies just keep jostlin' up de fire 'cause we are goin' to have fishes in no time!

(He starts to leave).

Don't you go away now!

(He is gone).

BRER FOX. Well, now ain't dis a fine kettle of fish . . . I sure wish I had somethin' to munch on while I was waitin' . . . don't you, Brer Bear?

BRER TARRYPIN. Psst! . . . Psst!

(He motions for Brer Fox to step over).

More strange doin's goin' 'round dis old mill pond den *most* folks know.

Brer Fox. You don't mean it.

Brer Tarrypin. But I know, an' de lizards know . . . an' de bullfrogs know . . . we all know 'bout dat pot of gold.

Brer Fox and Brer Bear. Gold? Gold? What pot of gold?

Brer Tarrypin. De pot of gold down on de bottom of de pond . . . standin' right under where de moon is settin' . . . sssh . . . Here comes Brer Rabbit back . . . don't you say a word!

Brer Rabbit *(Entering with a net).* Here's de net . . . now for dat moon!

Brer Fox. Gimme dat net!

Brer Bear. Gim*me* dat net!

(Brer Bear and Brer Fox tug and pull on the net. Brer Fox grabs the net and jumps over the back of the bridge. Brer Bear jumps after him, ripping off his coat).

Brer Rabbit. You had better hurry an' get de net over dat moon.

Brer Fox. It just keeps slippin' through de holes . . . get away, Brer Bear, you're scarin' de moon away . . . stand still, moon!

Brer Bear. It ain't me scarin' de moon, it's you with your big mouth!

Brer Fox. Who you callin' a big mouth? . . . you tub of lard!

Brer Bear. Hey, Big Mouth . . . who you callin' a tub of lard . . .!

Brer Fox. I'm callin' you a tub of lard . . . Goober brain!

Brer Bear. I'll teach you to call me dose things!

(There is a big thud and Brer Fox screams. They appear under the bridge yelling and screaming and hitting each other over the head. They climb over the reeds and Brer Bear chases Brer Fox around the stage, over the bridge and out. All the time they're under the net and Brer Fox is getting hit with the club. Brer Rabbit is doubled over with laughter as are the others).

Brer Tarrypin. Dere dey goes, a whoopin' an' a hollerin' right through de briar patch!

Brer Coon. Looks like old Brer Fox has got himself a whole bunch of new troubles!

Miss Meadows. He won't have time to pester *us* anymore.

Brer Rabbit. It's gonna be mighty boresome without de prankin' an' trickin' . . . especially now dat Brer Fox has himself other troubles to worry on.

Miss Meadows. You said you'd sworn off de trickin', Brer Rabbit.

Brer Rabbit. I know it . . . but dat was when I was sickly with de Mopes . . . but now de Mopes is gone! . . . Dey *are* gone, ain't dey, Aunt Mammy-Bammy?

Aunt Mammy. Lord child, you never had de Mopes to begin with . . . all you had was a touch of de gloppy gloomies.

Brer Rabbit. You mean all dat worryin' was just worryin' about de worryin', Aunt Mammy?

Aunt Mammy. Ain't no one alive dat can out-smart you, Brer Rabbit. You found dat out today. Why you're de smartest critter in dese parts . . . so quit your worryin' an' do what you gotta do. If it's prankin' an' caperin' you gotta do most . . . den do it . . . an' start livin' de life! Dat goes for de rest of you, too. Live de life you got . . . You only got one in dis world, so make de best of it. Why, de only worryin' you should have is how to make tomorrow better den today!

(From off stage comes whooping and hollering as Brer Fox enters chasing Brer Bear with a club).

Aunt Mammy. See dat's what I mean . . . you can't tell from one minute to de next how de events is gonna switch aroun' dese parts.

(She laughs).

Brer Rabbit. Turn on dat music playin' contraption of yours, Sis Buzzard, an' let's start livin' de life now!

(She turns on her radio and lively music comes on. Sis and Brer Coon start to dance as do Miss Goose and Brer Tarrypin).

Brer Fox. Stop! Brer Bear, dis is our big chance . . . let's get us dat rabbit dis time for good!

(They start chasing Brer Rabbit. Aunt Mammy just laughs away.

They freeze in running positions, the music stops as Aunt Mammy speaks).

Aunt Mammy *(To the audience)*. You all just might as well go on home, 'cause dere ain't no end to dis . . . an' dere ain't never gonna be. Don't worry, dey'll be all right. Lordy! Dey is just livin' de life!

(Laughs). (The stage again comes alive as the curtain falls).